iPHONE 11 PRO USERS GUIDE

Mastering The iPhone 11 Pro: A Complete Step by Step Guide For Beginners and Seniors

TECHY JAMES

Techy James

iPhone 11 Pro Users guide

COPYRIGHT

All rights reserved

NO PART OF THIS BOOK SHOULD BE REPRODUCED, REPRINTED OR STORED IN ANY ELECTRONIC SYSTEM WITHOUT THE PERMISSION BY THE AUTHORS

Copyright (c) Techy James 2019

Techy James

iPhone 11 Pro Users guide

Table of Contents

Introduction 1

Overview to the new iPhone 11 Pro 2

How To Begin Setting Up Your iPhone 11 Pro .. 8

How to Set Up Your iPhone 11 Pro As New 10

What's New With iOS 13 11

First things to do After Setup: New iPhone 11 Features 16

Physical Features of iPhone 11 Pro 24

How to Power ON and OFF Your iPhone 25

iPhone 11 Pro Gestures 27

How to Activate Siri 28

How to access Lock screen 29

How to access Control Centre 29

How to access Search Bar 29

How the Face ID and Passcode Works 30

How to Change the Wallpaper 31

How to Use Control Centre 32

How to customize the control centre 34

How to use Siri on iPhone 11 series 35

Common Built-in Apps 36

The Appstore: How to Use It 39

How to Organize Apps 40
   Settings 41
iPhone 11 Pro Tricks and Tips: 20 Things you
don't know 43
Conclusion 52

Techy James

iPhone 11 Pro Users guide

Introduction

If you just purchased a new iPhone 11, iPhone 11 Pro or iPhone 11 Pro Max, there are just few steps you'll need to get it set up and begin using your iPhone. We will sail you via these processes from the 'Hello' to the Apple's built-in apps like mail, Facetime, Messages and more new features. Also, you get to know how to operate the new iOS 13 and how to get music, movies, games, apps and many more right on your iphone. If this is your 1st Apple phone, congratulations and welcome to our family.

After unboxing, your new iPhone 11 Pro is very much ready to set it up. You will be welcome with a friendly 'Hello.' From there, you can now proceed to set it up or move data from iPhone or Andriod phone or even from a Windows phone to your new iPhone. Don't worry, you will get to know everything, just keep reading! In this guide, I'm going to show you a complete beginners guide to your new iPhone 11 Pro. This will also work for iPhone XS and iPhone X. I'm going to work you through how to use your iPhone from start to finish. Everything from what's in the box to how to use the features of your phone, things you need to turn ON and turn off, so sit back and relax because this guide is going to make you an iPhone expert.

Overview to the new iPhone 11 Pro

Apple finally unveils the long awaited iPhone 11, 11 Pro and 11 Pro Max. This new iPhone actually came with pretty much improvements. The first of which is right there at the back – Apple's all-new-camera system. The camera has an ultrawide feature that lets you to see more of your photos and videos. It also has 2X telephotoism that allows 40% more light. The cameras now have night modes (a feature commonly seen on Andriod phones). This allows you to take decent photos in a really low-light situations without having to use the flash. However, if you decide to use the flash, it is 30% brighter than before. You can access video quickly from the camera without going direct into the video mode. (check subsequent pages for directions). The camera is also bumped up with 12 megapixels compared to 7 megapixel on last year iPhone. This allow for wider angle selfies when you turn the phone into landscape.

There is also a new feature that Apple calls SLOFIES; with this, you can record your selfies in slow motions. Apple has claimed that the new iPhone 11 series is more water resistant than the previous series. The battery of iPhone 11 series last 4—5 hours more than iPhone Xs and Xs Max. Though I'm a little skeptical about these claims because it sounds too good to be true but Apple confirmed that they were able to do it via the super retina XDR display which is 15% more efficient than the previous models. The battery is also composed of the All-new A13 bionic chip which not only has a 20% faster CPU but also uses 40% more glass power.

Additionally, the iPhone 11 series all have improved sound system with spatial audio.

The sound is thus a bit clearer and more dynamic. Another new feature that Apple didn't talk much is the new U1 chip – An ultraband chip that gives the iPhone spatial awareness. So with this chip, you will be able to point your device towards another iPhone, and *Airdrop* will automatically prioritize the device to enable you share files in a faster way.

So with all these exceptional features, iPhone 11, 11 Pro and 11 Pro Max are the talk of the tech world!

Best Audiobooks For You!

- **Apple Watch Guide For Beginners (https://adbl.co/2Omz5PN)**
- **2018/2019 Amazon Alexa Guide (https://adbl.co/2MmxneO)**
- **2018 Amazon Echo Dot Guide (https://adbl.co/2In5hyE)**

- 2019 Amazon Echo Made Easy (https://adbl.co/2oW7Fp6)
- 2019 Amazon Echo Show Manual (https://adbl.co/2Vgpbk4)
- Amazon Fire TV Made Easy (https://adbl.co/2LPKfuP)
- Cricut Explore Air 2 Guide for Beginners (https://adbl.co/2LO3QeD)

Best Deals For You!

- Fully Unlocked Black Apple iPhone XR (https://amzn.to/31QloMR)
- Fully Unlocked Black Apple iPhone 8 (https://amzn.to/2ojjtBT)
- New Apple Watch Series 5 (https://amzn.to/2MeoML6)
- Silver Apple Watch Series 4 (https://amzn.to/2IFCENx)
- Cricut Explore Air 2 Machine (https://amzn.to/2AGPmqP)
- Cricut Explore Bundle (https://amzn.to/33bN1At.

Recommended Books For You

- Cricut Explore Air 2 Machine Guide (mybook.to/cricut)

- **Amazon Echo Show Beginners Guide 2019/2020 (getbook.at/Echoshow)**
- **Amazon Locker Guide For Beginners (getbook.at/Amazonlockerguide)**
- **Samsung Galaxy S10 Beginners Guide (mybook.to/SamsungGalaxyS10)**
- **Amazon Echo Dot For Beginners (mybook.to/EchodotMadeEasy.**

After unboxing, the following accessories can be seen:

a. Wall adapter plug
b. USB
c. Apple ear plugs for listening to music etc. The headphones have volumes up and down and you can use the centre, to activate Siri and ask your questions.
d. Apples 3-5mm jack adapter.

How To Begin Setting Up Your iPhone 11 Pro

- Tap the side button to start your iPhone
- Click *'slide to set up'* and gently slide your index finger across the screen.
- Choose your language choice
- Choose your region or country
- Choose any Wifi network. If your area is not within the Wifi network range, then you can do it later. Choose *'cellular'* instead. At this stage, you can decide to use *'Automatic setup'* to continue the setup of your new iPhone, using the same settings and passcode of your previous iPhone (if you had any). If you wish to continue the setup manually, then continue with the steps below:

- Click *'continue'* after going through Apple's Data and Privacy information.
- Click 'Enable Location Services.' If you don't want this function to be enabled, choose 'skip location services'
- Next, set up your face ID: first, position your face very well on your camera frame, then gently tilt your head in a slow manner to complete the circle.
- Enable a passcode: you can use a standard 6-digit passcode or a 4-digit passcode by tapping 'passcode options'
- A new window will pop up with options like: *if you want to set up as a new iPhone; if you want to restore*

from a backup or if you wish to transfer data from Android.

How to Set Up Your iPhone 11 Pro As New

If you are just a newbie in the world of iPhone or you don't wish to move over the data in your previous iPhone, then you can set it as 'new'

- Select *'set up as New iPhone'*
- Put your password and Apple ID. If you don't have anyone, then you can create a new one. Just click, "Don't have an Apple ID?" and navigate through the steps.
- Tap 'Agree' on the Apple's terms and condition after reading it.
- Set up your 'Apple pay' followed by your 'iCloud keychain'
- Set up your 'Siri' and 'Hey Siri'

- Click 'send diagnostic information to apple'
- Click on 'display zoom' for more visual accessibility.
- Finish the setup by tapping 'Get started'

What's New With iOS 13

a. Dark Mode: This feature has finally arrived on the iOS 13. This dynamic feature implies unique wallpapers that change between dark and light when the sun rises or sets. Photos, Notes, Messages and other nature apps all come with their built-in support for dark mode.

b. Apple Maps: Apple has really faced tough times with Apple maps. However, this feature will be available for all by the end of 2019 or early next year.

c. Air drop: The iOS 13.1 present in the iPhone series activates the UI chip. With this, you can point from one UI chip device to another one in order to Airdrop files. Very cool!

d. Privacy and Security: The iOS 13 has many privacy and security features. It has a system-wide location tracking protection. If given permission to use your location always, the iOS will give you all the reports in a detailed manner. Apple will soon introduce 'sign-in with Apple.' This makes use of Face ID without showing any of your particulars. The sign-in with Apple also works well over the web.

e. Homekit: This is another wonderful Apple feature that analyses video. With this app, Apple will locally analyse your video data after which, it will upload onto your icloud. All the icloud accounts have 10 days of free services. Logitech among others are brands that will support this new feature. This HomeKit support will also be available for 'routers' meaning that, it can 'fire wall off' accessories using brands like Spectrum, Eero and Linksys.

f. Messages: Photos and names can easily be shared with iOS 13. This implies that the recipient of your message will get your photo and name whenever you text the person. Memoji has more options including accessories and makeup such as

AiriPods, hats and monocles. All these memojis also have a sticker pack that can be used in messages. Any device with an A9 or more can support the memoji stickers, thus it is more accessible than ever.

g. Cameras and Photos: Photos and cameras have many features in the iOS 13. It has new portrait lightening effects, thus you can easily decrease/increase the light intensity. Photos posses a new photo-editing interface. All you need to do is just to tap on it and drag (You can then adjust it). Also there are new tools for editing like noise reduction on the iOS 13. This new photo interface is also seen on videos. And for the very 1st time, videos can be rotated. The iOS 13 has a new way to navigate photos in iOS 13.

h. AirPods: Siri now has the ability to read through incoming messages and with your Airpods, you can easily and directly respond to it. There's no need of saying 'Hey siri' in order to reply. This works very well with apps that supports sirikit.

i. Audio sharing: This new feature enables you to transfer your audio to another device or phone so they can also hear the audio you're listening to.

j. HomePod: there is now a support for HomePod; therefore, you can easily move your audio directly to your homepod. This can be done automatically once your homepod is near your iPhone.

First things to do After Setup: New iPhone 11 Features

We will start by showing you the first things to do when you get your iphone 11. Importantly, we will look at the new features of this great device.

    a. Camera: Obviously, your iPhone 11 or 11 pro has incredibly new camera lenses that you can actually swipe back and forth. Even, the videos, you can as well switch the camera lenses. And what you may not know (its kind of a hidden feature) is that you can press and drag the camera button to the right if you want to record your videos. This saves your time of opening the video gesture.

    b. Silence Unknown Calls: This is a great feature present on your iPhone

11. You can use it to silence any calls that are coming in from unknown callers, spams or scams. To turn this off, go to 'settings' app > phone section > toggle the 'silence unknown callers' ON. This will now make only people that you have on your contact list or those that know you personally to contact you thus, saving you from headaches of spam/scam calls. I definitely recommend turning that feature 'ON' as one of the first things that you do.

c. Setting Up Dark Mode: One of the heavy features I want to show you has to do with the new 'DARK MODE" on the iphone 11 and 11 pro. To activate it, simply swipe down into the control centre and activate the dark mode. This changes everything to a darker background. That way, it's easier on the eyes and even easier to read at night. This is a great way to ensure that your eyes adjust to light. Another important thing is how to use the timer to set your dark and light modes respectively.

- First, navigate to the settings app and open it. Scroll down to the 'Display and Brightness'. Click on it. You will see 'light and dark' modes. By default, 'Automatic' is turned off (let's say you want light during the day and 'dark mode' during the night hours):
- Click the 'Automatic', it will toggle to 'ON'; you will set the

option 'light until sunset' – this means that during the day, you will see the light background and in the night, it will automatically change to dark mode. It's incredible.

- Now, if you click on the 'options,' you can set up the 'custom schedule' where you can change the exact time for this change but I prefer the 'Automatic'

d. Install Emergency SOS:

- Navigate to the 'settings' application.

- Scroll down to 'Emergency SOS' (By default, if you press and hold the volume buttons and side button at the same time, it will automatically activate the 'Emergency SOS.' However, not everyone will be able to remember this step. So I will encourage you to do this.

- On the Emergency SOS page, toggle 'call with side button' ON. This will automatically activate emergency services. You can call all.

With this activated, you can press the side buttons 5 times and you will be automatically connected so it's highly recommended for everyone.

e. Optimize Battery Charging:

- Navigate to settings > Battery. We have 'Battery health' as an option. Click on it

- Move to 'optimized battery charging' (what this does is your iphone will automatically detect when you need to charge your phone or remove it.

- Enable the option.

6. Activate Low Data Usage

- Navigate to settings > cellular > cellular data options > low data mode > toggle it 'ON'. This will limit your daily data usage.

7. Close Used Tabs Automatically:

- Go to settings

- Scroll down to 'Safari' and click on it.

- Scroll down to 'close tabs' (By default, it's manually set)

- Click on it; you will see 'After one day,' 'After one week' and 'After one month.' I normally recommend 'After one day'

Best Audiobooks For You!
- Apple Watch Guide For Beginners (https://adbl.co/2Omz5PN)
- 2018/2019 Amazon Alexa Guide (https://adbl.co/2MmxneO)
- 2018 Amazon Echo Dot Guide (https://adbl.co/2In5hyE)
- 2019 Amazon Echo Made Easy (https://adbl.co/2oW7Fp6)
- 2019 Amazon Echo Show Manual (https://adbl.co/2Vgpbk4)
- Amazon Fire TV Made Easy (https://adbl.co/2LPKfuP)
- Cricut Explore Air 2 Guide for Beginners (https://adbl.co/2LO3QeD)

Best Deals For You!

- Fully Unlocked Black Apple iPhone XR (https://amzn.to/31QloMR)
- Fully Unlocked Black Apple iPhone 8 (https://amzn.to/20jjtBT)
- New Apple Watch Series 5 (https://amzn.to/2MeoML6)
- Silver Apple Watch Series 4 (https://amzn.to/2IFCENx)
- Cricut Explore Air 2 Machine (https://amzn.to/2AGPmqP)
- Cricut Explore Bundle (https://amzn.to/33bN1At.

Recommended Books For You

- Cricut Explore Air 2 Machine Guide (mybook.to/cricut)
- Amazon Echo Show Beginners Guide 2019/2020 (getbook.at/Echoshow)
- Amazon Locker Guide For Beginners (getbook.at/Amazonlockerguide)
- Samsung Galaxy S10 Beginners Guide (mybook.to/SamsungGalaxyS10

- **Amazon Echo Dot For Beginners (mybook.to/EchodotMadeEasy.**

Physical Features of iPhone 11 Pro

Before delving into the phone itself, we need to show you some other physical features of your new iPhone. On the front, you do have the screen, the speaker and the front camera.

On the side, you have the side buttons on the top right hand side of your phone.

On the otherside of the phone, there is a mute switch. When the switch is muted, it shows a 'RED'

Also, we have the volume (up and down) buttons. On the bottom, we do have the charging port and the speakers too.

How to Power ON and OFF Your iPhone

Now, I'm going to show you how to turn ON your phone, turn off your phone and as well as have emergency restart if there is a freezing or hanging of your phone.

Now the easiest way to turn ON your phone (if it has just been on sleep mode) is to just tap on the side button.

To turn off, just press the **side button** again and it will *'sleep'* the phone.

Another way to turn your phone 'ON' from the sleep mode is just by 'tapping' gently on the screen. It's actually recommended that you 'shut down' your phone at least once every month, because it refreshes your phone and prevents slow down.

To 'shut down' - hold the side button and then the 'volume up' button; it will automatically bring out a menu '**slide to power off**'. – slide and your phone is completely shutdown.

To turn ON again, gently press the side button, the apple logo comes out and it will become fully powered ON.

Now let's say that your phone automatically freezes, that you can't do any other thing on it; all you have to do is to force 'restart' of your phone.

- Press the volume up, then the volume down and hold the side buttons for 10 seconds.
- This will force restart of your device without telling you to swipe.

iPhone 11 Pro Gestures

Now, I'm going to show you all of the different gestures for your iPhone. We start with the 'lock screen'

- To switch quickly between 2 different applications, use the ball on the bottom; all you have to do is swipe over to and fro. This will take you to the next application.
- If you want to get an app you have opened relatively quickly or to see some of the apps at the background, just hold the bar on the bottom of the screen with a finger and pull it up. Hold it for a second.
- You will see all the different apps you have opened. Just tap

anyone you want and you will get the application.
- To delete any of the background apps:
- Tap firmly on the app, a red delete icon will appear on each of the apps, touch this icon or simply swipe it up.

How to Activate Siri

To activate siri;

- Tap and hold the side button and you will access siri just like that.
- Another way to do this is by saying: 'Hey siri'

How to access Lock screen

- The easy way to do this is by gently swiping from the top left of your screen.

How to access Control Centre

- Use a finger to swipe down from the top right of your screen,

How to access Search Bar

- Use a finger to swipe down from the centre of the screen.
- With the search bar activated, you can search for email, messages, apps etc.

How the Face ID and Passcode Works

Face ID works by scanning your face and allowing you to have access directly on your phone.

To activate this:

- Tap on settings
- Scroll down to 'Face ID and Passcode'
- Enter a passcode you can remember
- A window appears with description 'Use Face ID for': There are 4 functions there.
- Enable any of your choices. If you want all, tap on each of them to become activated.
- If you wish to reset your Face ID, click on 'Reset Face ID.' It will automatically begin the process. Follow the steps.

- Apple shows you how to get this completed.

Also, if you wish to change your passcode, tap on 'change passcode'

On the same window, you can see what you need to allow access when the screen is locked. For instance, if you don't want people to read your message or notifications; just turn off 'Today view' and 'Recent Notifications'

How to Change the Wallpaper

So I will show you how to change the wallpapers of your iPhone.

To change your wallpaper;

- Gently click on 'settings'
- Scroll down to 'wallpaper' and click on it.

- You can choose a new wallpaper right there on the top.
- Click 'set'
- You will now decide if the wallpaper should be used for both the lockscreen and homescreen.

How to Use Control Centre

Again, to access your control centre, you only need to swipe down from the top right of your screen. There are varieties of different icons and we are going to go over each of them and see how to customize your control centre as well.

- At the first left hand corner, you will see *airplane mode, cellular, wifi and Bluetooth.*

- When 'Airplane mode' is tapped, it turns off cellular data and Bluetooth.
- At the top right, you will see the music icon where you can 'pause'or 'continue' your music, videos etc. it's an easy control area for any app that uses an audio functionality.
- The next is the *'Lock rotation.'* This locks your phone on the portrait orientation when it is enabled.
- Next to that is *'Do not Disturb'* – when enabled, you will not get phone calls, app notifications or messages. However, if this functionality is 'ON', then what it means is you will be notified

by a sound, buzz or vibrations when you get a text message.
- Next is the *'Brightness settings'* – you can turn it up or down as well as the *'volume settings'*
- If you press the brightness icon a little bit harder, it will bring out the *'true tone'* and *'night shift'*.
- *'Screen mirroring'* allows you to mirror the screen of your phone on another device such as laptop or a projector.

How to customize the control centre

- Navigate to settings
- Click on *'control centre'*
- Tap on 'customize control centre'
- Go to 'more control' and tap on any feature of your choice.

- It will automatically be added into your control centre.

How to use Siri on iPhone 11 series

As earlier stated, siri can be activated by firmly tapping the side button or just say 'Hey, Siri.' These are some of the questions you can ask siri:

- What's the weather like in California?
- Send a text message to Chris
- Siri response: What do you want to say? You: *type your message now.*
- To know many other questions to ask siri, do this:
- You: what can I ask you?

- Siri: It brings out a lot of suggestions such as phone calls, face time, apps, messages, calendar etc. This gives you idea of the questions siri is willing to answer you.

Common Built-in Apps

I am going to show you some of the other apps that comes installed on your new iPhone 11. I will be showing each of them but I will recommend that you experiment with each of them yourself so that you will really see how they work.

    a. Calendar: It allows you to add events into your phone.
- Tap on the day and click the '+' sign.
- Choose the time of the event
- You are good to go.

b. Photos: this will show you all the photos you have taken with your phone. You can scroll through to see them.

c. Camera: You can use it either in the portrait or landscape mode. To snap a picture;
   - You can use the volume up button to take photos or press the white button on the bottom as well.
   - You can press the flash feature to turn ON or OFF. You can turn ON/OFF the HDR photos depending on the quality you're really looking for. You can also turn ON the timer as well. Even filters can be added depending on the one you're looking for.

- In addition to this, you have the ability to zoom in/out the camera and change the focus point of your photo just by tapping on where you like your camera to focus.
- If you swipe across the camera screen, you can take video recording (slow motion video is great for sports)

d. Maps: All you have to do is:
- Put an address in the search bar
- Click 'Go' and you will get step by step directions just like the GPS.

e. Weather: This app will show you the weather condition of your current location

f. News: This will show you the latest trending in the globe.

g. Notes: You can keep track of what you're thinking just by typing a note and saving it on your phone. You can also draw on this 'Note' as well. When you have finished, just click 'Done'and you're good to go.

The Appstore: How to Use It

I am going to show you how to use the appstore to download additional apps on your device.

- First, click on the 'Appstore'
- You can scroll through all the suggested apps
- You can go to the 'Great on iPhone 11'
- You will see good apps you would probably want to download like the Netflix, twitter and the rest.

Another great way of getting good apps is to go to the Apps tab and scroll down to 'Top free'

- This will give a pretty information about all the apps you want to download such as: Youtube, Instagram, Facebook , Messenger etc.

How to Organize Apps

Use these steps to organizing your apps:

- Press and hold firmly any app of your choice
- The apps will enter into wiggle mode
- To move, press and drag the app to different locations of your choice

- If you want to delete an app, just click on the small 'X' sign on top of the app.
- Then click 'Done' to finalize your action.

Finally, if you want to organize one/two apps into a folder;

- Drag the app onto another and a folder will be created automatically.

Settings

There are a lot of settings in your iphone 11. I am going to do a brief overview of the settings;

- Click on 'settings'
- You will see your Name, Apple ID, icloud, itune

Appstore

When clicked, you will be able to reset your Apple ID and change things about icloud etc.

Notifications

When clicked, you could see *'show previous > when unlocked'*- this means that if your phone is locked, no body can read your message or notifications till it is unlocked.

iPhone storage

This shows you all the different apps on your phone and the amount of space they are taking. It will help you to get rid of them if they are not useful.

To enable:

- Click on General > iPhone storage
- Simply tap on the app.
- Scroll below and click on the 'Delete app'

Those are the main settings on the iPhone. You can play around other ones and see things for yourself.

iPhone 11 Pro Tricks and Tips: 20 Things you don't know

a. How to go to the Homescreen Faster: if you wish to move to the homescreen from the widget screens or lockscreens or any other homescreens, then follow these steps:
- Touch your fingers on your phone gesture area
- Gently flick it up

b. How to Switch Between Apps Faster:
- Touch a finger at the gesture area on the bottom of your device
- Swipe gently from the left direction to the right side to open the previous app
- Swipe gently from the right side to the left for the next app.

c. How to open the Multitasking App Switcher:

You have to use the new gesture when you wish to quickly swipe back and forth of multiple apps. Do the following:

- Put the finger on your gesture area on the bottom of your iPhone
- Slightly swipe it up (never flick)

d. How to Quit Apps Forcely on iPhone:

This is very easy; you can forcibly quit all your apps with a single swipe up in your app switcher tray.

- Put your finger on the gesture area.
- Slightly swipe it up
- Pause for a while. Don't raise the finger up immediately. Just pause.
- Now gently lift your finger
- Swipe firmly on the app card. Voom! It's gone. Anytime you're on the killing mode, many battery draining apps can be removed.

e. How to Enter Reachability Mode:

Unlike other features, this gesture need to be set up first. Follow these steps:

- Tap on settings from your homescreen
- Click on General > Accessibility
- Toggle the 'Reachability' gesture to 'ON'

Once it is set up:

- Touch a finger on the gesture area on the bottom of your device
- Gently swipe it down

f. How to Turn ON your device
- Firmly tap and hold the side button for few seconds

g. How to Wake or Sleep your iPhone
- Tap the side button

h. How to disable Face ID Temporarily

- First, ensure the screen of your iPhone is off
- Tap and hold your side button with any of the volume button

i. How to Open Apple Pay
- Tap the side button two times

j. How to Get Accessibility Shortcuts
- Tap three times on your side buttons

k. How to Easily Take a Screenshot
- Tap on the side button with the volume up button.

l. How to Reboot or Reset iPhone
- Tap volume up
- Tap volume down
- Tap and hold your side button.

m. How to Navigate iPhone 11 series Homescreen
- The homescreen is the home base of your iPhone from where

everything starts.' You can navigate to the homescreen by simply tapping 'home button.' If your device is locked with a passcode, then do the following below:

- Tap your home button
- Put the 6 digit/4 digit or alphanumeric password.
- If the iPhone is locked with Touch ID, then put your registered finger on your home button.
- Tap the home button afterwards.
- If your phone is locked with Face ID, then do the following:
- Tap or 'raise' to wake it
- Glance at the screen in a portrait mode

- Swipe up with your finger from the screen bottom to unlock
n. How to switch Homescreens

 Your device can have more than one homescreen. With this, you can have numerous apps that would fit on a page. To switch your homescreens, do the following:
 - Use a finger to swipe from the right to the left side to enter the next homepage
 - To go back to the previous homepage, swipe a finger from the left to right
 - Tap on the 'home button' to navigate to the main homepage.

o. How to Quickly Switch Apps Via Home Screen

 It can be very tiresome launching an app, going back to your homescreen and re-launching the first app again. That's why iPhone offers a very fast way to navigate between recently used apps. To do this, follow these steps:

- Double-click on your home button/slide a finger from the device bottom in the case of Face ID-compatible iPhone.
- Move to the app you wish to use (they are in sequential order)
- Click on the app screen to switch to it.

p. How to Get Spotlight Search

This built-in feature can be used to easily find information on apps. This is not only limited to apps that came with your device but it's inclusive of apps that can be downloaded from your

Appstore. With this feature, you can find things like songs, emails, contacts and much more.

- Tap a finger on the homescreen (in between two apps works best)
- Swipe a finger down to see the spotlight search space
- Type in your request
- Click on the result you want.

Conclusion

I hope you found this guide valuable – How to use your new iPhone 11 Pro. We put this guide together to show you step by step approach of how everything works. Don't forget to share the guide with somebody.

Thank you for reading.

You can contact us via mail (bestauthor02@gmail.com). We are always available to help you become a tech-savvy individual.

Best Audiobooks For You!

- Apple Watch Guide For Beginners (https://adbl.co/2Omz5PN)
- 2018/2019 Amazon Alexa Guide (https://adbl.co/2MmxneO)
- 2018 Amazon Echo Dot Guide (https://adbl.co/2In5hyE)
- 2019 Amazon Echo Made Easy (https://adbl.co/2oW7Fp6)
- 2019 Amazon Echo Show Manual (https://adbl.co/2Vgpbk4)
- Amazon Fire TV Made Easy (https://adbl.co/2LPKfuP)
- Cricut Explore Air 2 Guide for Beginners (https://adbl.co/2LO3QeD)

Best Deals For You!

- Fully Unlocked Black Apple iPhone XR (https://amzn.to/31QloMR)
- Fully Unlocked Black Apple iPhone 8 (https://amzn.to/2ojjtBT)
- New Apple Watch Series 5 (https://amzn.to/2MeoML6)
- Silver Apple Watch Series 4 (https://amzn.to/2IFCENx)
- Cricut Explore Air 2 Machine (https://amzn.to/2AGPmqP)
- Cricut Explore Bundle (https://amzn.to/33bN1At)

Recommended Books For You

- Cricut Explore Air 2 Machine Guide (mybook.to/cricut)

- Amazon Echo Show Beginners Guide 2019/2020 (getbook.at/Echoshow)
- Amazon Locker Guide For Beginners (getbook.at/Amazonlockerguide)
- Samsung Galaxy S10 Beginners Guide (mybook.to/SamsungGalaxyS10
- Amazon Echo Dot For Beginners (mybook.to/EchodotMadeEasy)

Made in the USA
Las Vegas, NV
02 February 2022